The Heartland Review

Spring 2018

Vol. 18 No. 2

Cover
Janus (watercolor)
by
Jo Friel

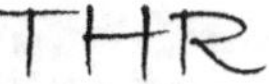

Elizabethtown Community and Technical College
600 College Street Road
Elizabethtown, KY

ISSN 2473-9545
ISBN 978-0-9996868-3-6

The Heartland Review is an imprint of The Heartland Review Press. Views expressed in items appearing herein are those of the author or artist. Publication of materials does not reflect the views or opinions of Elizabethtown Community and Technical College or KCTCS.

The Heartland Review is published with generous funds from KCTCS and Elizabethtown Community and Technical College president's office, as well as donations from friends, contributors, and contest entrants. We want to thank everyone for the continued support of this journal.

To submit go to:

The Heartland Review Submittable

To subscribe, visit our website

$12.00/issue $20.00/year

Contributors

Editor's Notes

Many thanks to everyone who has contributed to the success of our 2018 Joy Bale Boone Poetry Prize, especially our judges Nickole Brown and Jessica Jacobs. THR is honored to offer a place for poets and writers to share their voices that together effect a balm for the soul of the world.

Following are Nickole & Jessica's notes for the winners:

First Place: Heidi Seaborn

"What I Knew" manages to hold two realities at once: that of a young high-school girl in Seattle and of the simultaneous war in Vietnam, melding together the green and mud of both places while comparing their violences great and small. Most surprising is the ending, set on the Fourth of July, when we have a nod to the beauty of such terror, that collective and disturbing "ahhhh." This poem, deeply internal and moving with surprising associative leaps and overlapping remembrances, holds two vastly different worlds with a quick and limber dexterity and is effective as a poem of witness in its firm grasp on the speaker's personal experience.

Second Place: Elaine Fowler Palencia

"The Buttonhook" delights like a child's fable might—it begins with that gate unlocked with a tarnished buttonhook and takes us through a series of imaginings both unpredictable and haunted, ending with a note one could not have foreseen in those first few stanzas. The imagery is historical and textured, and some of the images (like "tapers burning down/like young girls blazing with tuberculosis") deserve a special nod.

Third Place: Maggie Blake Bailey

How many times have you been on your way to somewhere difficult, your mind gripped with such anticipation that it transforms everything in your path into a symbol of your foreboding? "A Flood Like That Would Be Better" powerfully captures this experience: a wake of buzzards are "hunched like old women…heavy shouldered/ and menacing," the speaker a lobster in slow-boiling water, dreaming of the flood that might sweep it all away, rescued by that devastation from the dread and threat of the mother's house.

Our cover art is special as well for *Janus* is the work of Jo Friel the 2018 Central Kentucky Art Guild's Artist of the year. Also a member of the Kentucky Watercolor Society, Jo has been an aspiring artist since her earliest memories. With both parents artists, Jo says "I naturally thought that art was the 'thing to do.'" She prefers watercolor, "the most difficult medium I've found" and enjoys the "challenge of painting en plein air when the weather is agreeable."

Happy Spring!
mk

First Place 2018 Joy Bale Boone Poetry Prize

Heidi Seaborn

What I Knew

about the war I knew
from the tv black & white & grey.
Knew nothing about green
blotting the sun jungle green
slick as seaweed green
just-shipped-out green khaki
camouflage green eyes seeing nothing
no more green.

Knew mud & rain. A
Seattle girl knows mud & rain.
But not seeping rain raining
in pores swamping your guts rain.
Not mud that sucks   swallows
boots legs to the knee mud
mud birthing leeches malaria mines.

Knew a year seemed to take forever
from one birthday to the next. Not time
measured in days marked alive.
Each day a birth a death another day. Fear.

Knew fear of walking
past the line of sixth-grade boys
whistles & barks.
My enemies were all noise
bluster, hope & pimples
& the fights bloodied noses broken
fingers wrestling in the playground.
Once a boy threw a can
of gasoline on another & a match.

Growing up in Jet City I knew Blue
Angel Super Sonic scorched earth
screaming jets. But no bombs
planes people fell
out of my chalk-scrawled skies.

I'd lie on the tall snake green
incandescent rice paddy green grass
next to the post office
on the 4th of July & watch the
night explode. Feel rocket
vibrations, hum of our collective ahhhh.

Michele Parker Randall
Phenomenology

fickle wind blows smoke
in every direction flicks
bits of ash onto skin
which I rub in
when the cane fields burn
I am the cane
the rabbits caught in burlap sacks
the snakes and rats fleeing the scene
the night that is dry enough to burn
wet enough to contain
the match and stalk
the smoke and rubble
you ask me to pack it up
and give it all to you
for a career-making-case-study
every god-forsaken moment

I write down
I am the cane offered up
and left behind for seed
the studied and the medium

I am framed with raw edges
showing as art

Janice Fuller
Alfresco

His chiseled features
intensified but softened
as he balanced above her,
then gently settled on her body.
Dressed only in their t-shirts,
jeans beside them in the grass
still green but spread
with crackling scarlet leaves.

A risk well worth
the effort on the short walk
through the woods. They knew
their discovery by the hikers
would verify the unlikely choice
they'd made. These two predictable
lovers always followed rules,
now grabbed the impulse,
laid down in open-air
for anyone to see, a signal
that their love was real
and changed them.

George Drew
A Story No One Else Can Tell

Imagine, in the summer of 1955, a boy of eleven,
a Mississippi boy born and raised, was headed north
to New York State and his paternal grandparents' house
on the Hudson River, and at the same time
a young boy of fourteen, a black Chicago boy,
was headed south to Mississippi and his uncle's house
on the Tallahatchie River, the same river
Billie Joe McAllister leapt into from the wooden bridge
that crosses it in Money, the town to which
the young black boy traveled that summer of 1955.

Might that young black boy and young white boy
have crossed paths within actual sight of each other
as one was coming to and one going from the Delta?

No one will ever know, but if such an intersection
of two souls isn't the stuff dreams are made of,
it is the stuff of stories no one else can tell;
and what no one can tell is that from one day late
in August in Mississippi in 1955 when the white man
who was that small white boy hears the word Tallahatchie,
a word that once was beautiful on his tongue and in his ears,
beautiful even in an ode to a suicide, it summons nothing
but black—black river, black sky and a black body
beaten and bloody and bound in barbed wire.

What that man can tell is that the young black boy
has been the unsuspecting mentor of the story,
of their story, a story that no one else can ever tell.

Melissa Hassard
Birds in Winter

She reheats coffee, slowpours the cream, thinks of him
drizzling away from her on a slow, early train
while muscle and tendon remind her of the night before,
the way they'd offered up their bodies to each other.

Midday, she chops mirepoix, starts a soup, watches
the window for winter birds tempted to a feeder,
thinks Life unto life but can't exactly say why.
Crows and squirrels hop closer to inspect.

The sky, heavy as porridge, warms to deep orange,
steam rises from the pot. Cardinals flicker
in the wet grass, too many to count, like the days
til his return. The soup begins to simmer.

A sparrow on the fenceline, patient as the rain,
a black spot on his chest like a fingerprint,
as if God touched him there, as if to say
You only think your heart lives here.

Honorable Mention 2018 Joy Bale Boone Poetry Prize

Elaine Fowler Palencia
What the Bonsai Thinks

the potted violets urge patience
in their soft patois
we must be grateful
for protection, they say

but I dream of blue waters

yes yes I know I am safer
than the insolent squirrel
robbing the birdfeeder under the eye
of the red-tailed hawk
safer than the robin
clinging to a snowy branch
as his nest shreds in winter gales

but I dream of mountains

it is true, they will never
make me into furniture
or cook and eat me
like the potted basil
I am their little joy

but I dream of wind and rain

when cut flowers arrive
for their brief, showy stay
one can only be kind
for after all, as far as I can tell
I am immortal
and may well be a god.

Richard Foerster
Watercress

To pick a crisp salad from the garbage of the past is no snap.
—Wallace Stevens

Did you find everything you were looking for?
the teen at the checkout asked as he scanned
the groupings I'd arranged on the belt.

No, I said, looking deep into his earnest face.
Sixteen perhaps, with lashes like a pasha's fan
and the downy bloom of a first beard,

he tightened his brow with concern,
making golden threads in his green eyes
unapproachably radiant . . . No fault of his,

still I complained the market doesn't stock
watercress, which a chef like me considers
essential for salads with Boston and romaine.

What's watercress? He was too young
to appreciate the nourishing appeal
of bitterness, a taste admittedly at odds

with youthful cravings, yet one a man
acquires almost in defiance—to ingest
the biting world and not succumb

to its poisons. The boy nodded and smiled,
all the while deconstructing my neat piles
for reassembly in some adolescent application

of chaos theory. A half-century his senior, childless
and lacking necessary morsels of wisdom
a parent needs to nurture with neglect and let

inexperience stumble on its way, I watched
my canvas sacks begin to brim with disorder,
eggs wedged in with canned tomatoes,

as if the boy were gathering a future, there
before him, raw ingredients of a harvested
past, and I knew to hold my tongue.

Brit Washburn
Regarding Star Gazer Lilies

Why would anyone bother with other flowers,
you ask, regarding a bouquet of stargazer lilies
blooming beside my bed, the most recent of several
you've brought to me these last months, their blooms
bright pink and speckled, edged in white, and named
for the direction they face: upward, toward the light.

Nights when you're away, their fragrance fills the room
and makes it feel less empty, and me less alone
as I drift off to sleep beneath linens I'll launder
in time for your return, leaving the flat sheet
untucked on your side so your feet can breathe--

a cloying analogy for the pains we must take
to prepare a space for one another--clean
and warm and welcoming, but not constrictive,
a delicate balance between opening and receiving
and allowing ourselves to want and need and yes,
attach, even, to have the full experience
of human love, including vulnerability,

for God, I believe, designed it so to humble us:
we were not made to outwit loss, to circumvent it,
but to observe and learn the way petals yellow and curl,
the way pollen falls from stamen and stains
the white bookcase, and water must be changed,
and stems must be clipped and still will wilt

eventually. But not yet. Why rush it? Why bother
with any other endeavor than this
practice of acceptance and commitment
which even the Buddhists admit can liberate us
from our own whim and weakness, our own fear.

Beauty makes it clear that we are here for this:
to give, to trust, to gaze at each other as though
we too were stars worth regarding.

Kevin J. McDaniel
At the Foot of a Mountain

In a reclusive cabin
where a wood stove hiccups
orange embers clothed
in gray ash coats,

the bottoms of my feet
feel bitter, raw air
circulating over every inch
of hard floor awash in

ghostly blue moonlight.
Through a window, I see
a lone yellow buckeye bend
in a boisterous wind

that makes me believe
it can bring down
the entire mountainside,
but I know spring

will come again on wings
of a gentler breeze that uplifts
saplings rooted sideways
in moonmilk.

Anne Williams
The Tallest Thing on the Mountain

*I*n June of 1988, I drove out of Indianapolis heading my favorite direction—west. Summer school classes over, my two daughters visiting my sister in Tucson in the company of my parents, this was the kind of trip I had long dreamed of: a journey across the plains and into the Mountain West—on my own schedule and for the first time in my life, all alone.

When I proposed this trip, driving from Indiana to Tucson for the family gathering that would take place there over July 4, my parents offered to pay for airfare instead. It was too dangerous, they insisted, for me to drive 1800 miles alone through that big empty landscape, and even more worrisome if my daughters were with me on the return trip.

"There's no telling what could happen to you three girls on the road all alone," my dad told me.

But I was newly-divorced after nearly twenty years and feeling independent. At some point in the annoying telephone conversations, I took a stand: "I'm leaving right after I turn in my grades. I'll meet you all in Tucson five days later."

I crossed the Indiana line into Illinois with a sense of adventure. I would begin by travelling west to Colorado then northwest to my parents' house outside Estes Park, empty now, while they were in Tucson. There I would give myself the gift of one day in the Front Range of the Rockies, a day all to myself in my favorite place before continuing on to Tucson and family responsibilities.

For most of my childhood in Kansas City, summer meant a trip to Colorado and the rising tension as we left the Welcome to Colorful Colorado sign behind and began to strain our eyes, each one of us hoping to be the first to see the mountains. Now I undertook the same challenge all alone, enjoying those shifty moments when the clouds looked like snow and the snow looked like clouds until that reliable grey-blue line emerged to define the long mass of the Rocky Mountains.

I left Boulder behind and gained elevation, breathing air I could taste, that tang of sage and spruce as fresh and pungent as biting into a pine needle. Familiar peaks appeared, Twin Sisters to the east, Longs to the west, and the steep slant of Hallett's straight ahead, differentiated against the azure sky.

The house stood high above the road, glass front gleaming in the late afternoon sun. I carried one of my suitcases up the long terraced incline from the driveway and onto the deck. Once inside, I built a fire and made coffee. Later, wrapped in a blanket, I lay in a deck chair under a spangled sky, listening to the coyotes until the chill and fatigue drove me to bed.

The next day, with no schedule to follow, I slept late, drank coffee, and read old newspapers my dad kept in the kindling box until the heat of the sun through the big windows reminded me that this day I'd looked forward to for so long was ticking away. I decided to drive up into Rocky Mountain National Park, just a mile or so from the house, and take the trail up Flat Top, one of a series of Front Range peaks in the park.

It seemed like an obvious choice. I'd been up Flat Top many times before, most recently a quick trip one afternoon with my brother that assured me I had plenty of time today. The nine-mile round trip, judged "strenuous" by trail guides, requires none of the technical skills necessary for some other nearby peaks. Most people in my family considered it a good walk.

From years of my father's admonitions, years of newspaper stories about unprepared hikers coming to bad ends, I knew to dress sensibly and to take a rain jacket. I followed that advice. The advice I ignored was his mountain mantra: get off the top by noon. Storms often moved in by early afternoon, bringing all kinds of weather including deadly lightning. "You don't want to be the tallest thing up there above tree line in a storm," he always said.

The sun created rainbows in the spray as I drove upward along the tumbling river. I parked at the far end of the big lot and made my way through the crowds of park visitors on the paved trail around Bear Lake, then cut off on the westward path toward the Flat Top trailhead. I breathed in the cool green air where lush fern and wild flowers flourish in the damp, sandy soil and little streams spill across the trail. I felt instantly at home.

It's always surprising how soon the sounds of human society fall away, even on a heavily-used trail such as the one to Flat Top. Hikers pass each other silently, with a nod or one raised hand, acts of preservation for the silence they seek here: a silence of birds—Clark's Nut Crackers, Chickadees, Steller's Jays—and of the wind through the spruce and the pine.

I set my pace to stay out of sight of others and began the work of gaining altitude, enjoying the feel of being on my own in the rugged landscape, the measured steps, and the unaccustomed attention to each breath.

I have never felt it especially important to make the summit of a climb. What I want, what I climb for, is to leave the trees behind. Once there, the world opens up. You can see forever, and it all glistens—water in a thin surface layer permeates and silvers everything. At one rocky switchback high on the Flat Top trail grows a hedge of columbine, a drift of blue reprised nowhere except in that high-country sky. Once past it, I have no need to go much higher. All I want is to stand alone in the heat of the sun with the icy breeze from the glaciers blowing through me. It feels like heaven.

That afternoon, however, my pleasure was fleeting. My vantage point at more than 12,000 feet showed black clouds moving swiftly toward me, and I understood that I couldn't stay. Still, I stood my ground and took it all in for just a moment. I memorized the rose and gold of the flowering tundra, the silhouette of the marmot atop a boulder, and the kestrel's cry. I might regret the brevity of my time here today, but all I could possibly take away was the elemental satisfaction of standing in this place once more.

Within minutes the wind was blowing hard, carrying first snow, then tiny fragments of ice that foretold the hail soon to follow. I untied my jacket from my waist, pulled it on and zipped it tight, then tried to use the drawstring in the hood to decrease the exposure of my face to the cutting ice particles-all the while walking downward. As I did, I waited for fear to take hold of me, to quicken my pulse; but I was surprised by my own coolness. I wasn't afraid, but I was acutely aware that I, alone, was responsible for getting myself down the trail safely.

Other hikers passed me, or I passed them, but without any acknowledgement at all: everyone was intent on the footing. As the hail, now marble-sized and falling like rain, began to accumulate, each step was treacherous. In a place where you must always set a foot deliberately, experience and instinct were not enough. I wanted to hurry but forced myself to slow, to adjust my pace downward in keeping with the conditions.

I could feel the force of the hail through my jacket, and my hood did little to protect my head from the buffeting. When I spotted a spruce with bottom branches far enough from the ground to allow me a space, I crawled under it, bent my head low to protect my face, and pushed my hands inside the elasticized cuffs of my jacket, trying to warm them. I was sitting in hailstones, deafened by the rattle of ice falling through the trees when some movement caught my attention.

A young man had dropped to his knees and was crawling into the remaining space beneath the spruce. Wearing only a tee shirt, jeans, and sneakers, his teeth were chattering so hard he could barely speak to ask permission to join me. For another fifteen minutes or so we crouched there. I tried to stay intent on the weather, to ignore him even though he attempted conversation. "I'm Ben. I came up from Denver this morning. To climb a mountain." He paused when I nodded in response, then tried again. "Where are you from?"

"Indiana." I left it at that. The noise of the hail made communication difficult, and besides, I didn't want to end up being responsible for this young man.

Ten minutes later, with the weather showing no sign of letting up, I could see that waiting any longer would be a mistake. Ben's arms were curled around his knees, his head resting on them. The back of his neck looked vulnerable, young; he must be about nineteen, I decided. Wherever he was from, he wasn't prepared for this situation. And I admitted to myself that he would have to continue down the mountain with me. When I spoke to him, he didn't seem to hear, so I scooted nearer, "Ben," I said loudly. "We have to go."

He shook his head, not even looking my way. "I can't go back out in the hail," he said, curling his arms tighter around his knees. He was shaking from the cold, and I remembered that shivering is a protective response. "Walking will help keep you warm," I told him, the very idea of warm sounding ridiculous, even to me. However, it must have appealed to him, for soon he was pushing himself out toward the trail where the hail was now at least three inches deep. We began to slip and slide downward, grasping at trees and brush for support.

About halfway to the trailhead, we confronted a series of stone ledges which had been just an outsized staircase on the way up, but now each step down to the next level included a frightening moment of uncertainty as I balanced on my left foot while the right sought stability on the iced stone below. When Ben finally made his way to the bottom ledge, his face was bleeding from the hail, his lips were blue, and his hands were so cold that he could barely hold onto his walking stick.

"You go ahead," he said. "Then you can send someone back for me." But I couldn't do it. Who would I send? And what would they find? He had to keep walking and I had no help to offer him but encouragement.

We made our way another mile or so, and as we lost elevation, the hail mixed with rain. Icy water dripped into my face from my hood; Ben's hair appeared to be frozen. Then, with no warning, from out of the trees on the right, another trail intersected ours. No marker identified it; I did not remember this fork from the trip up.

For a moment, I felt panic. Under normal circumstances, I would have been sure that ours was the main trail and traveled on without a second thought. But now any decision I made would be critical, and I paused, peering down the blurred passageway, hoping for something that would assure me of the way forward.

What I saw was a patch of bright orange moving our direction: a group of hikers. Three men with backpacks. After just a glance at us, one of them dropped his pack and pulled out a sweatshirt and then a pair of gloves. Instantly, it seemed, Ben's shirt was off and the sweatshirt on. Then gloves, then a plastic poncho. My own Gore Texjacket no longer repelled the rain but I was in no danger, so I shook my head at their offer of dry clothing and we travelled on together.

The trailhead lay at the bottom of a final steep decline, awash in a slushy mix of rain and hail deep enough to fill my low boots, already sodden and heavy. One of the men who had provided the clothing put an arm around Ben, who was still shaking violently. "I'll get you over to the Ranger's Station; it's not far down this next trail," he told him.

Ben's teeth chattered as he tried to refuse the help, but the rescuer would have none of it. "You're in hypothermia now," he said. "We'll pick you up bodily if you don't come along."

Ben raised a hand toward me and I nodded. The group disappeared into the trees without a backward glance, and I took my own direction, wading through slush that seemed thick as mud to my suddenly weak and shaky legs.

*

*M*y car sat nearly alone at the far end of the lot. With numb fingers I struggled to put the key into the icy lock, feeling relief wash over me when it turned and I was able to knock away enough snow and ice to open the door. I started the engine and waited for heat. The snow- covered windows created a dim white cave, and I thought of the moments beneath that spruce tree amid the barrage of hail and snow that cut through the thick cover of the branches. It came to me in a collage of icy blue needles, an image I seemed unable to turn away from.

When the engine began to produce heat, I slowly unzipped my jacket, amazed at how long it took my clumsy fingers to perform the task. The wet pieces of my clothing clung to each other, and when I was finally undressed, my skin was cold in a way I had never experienced. Cold clear into the core of me. I had left one suitcase in the car the night before, and I raided it now to find dry underwear and socks, some jeans, a long sleeved shirt, a cardigan sweater, and a pair of dressy flats. Slowly, painfully, as feeling returned to my fingers, I dragged fabric against my clammy skin, fit buttons into buttonholes, and worked my feet, numb as my fmgers, into the socks.

The heater was melting the snow from the windshield, and I wiped condensation away so that I could see where I had been. The mountains were gone, shrouded in a whiteness akin to nothingness. I wondered what it was like along that trail now, under the spruce and on the steep stretches. I wondered if anyone was still up there.

Snow was piling up in the parking lot, so I forced myself to start down the twisty road to the valley below where I knew the precipitation would probably change to rain. The trip was slow, low clouds obscuring the road, my hands on the steering wheel still shaky from cold and fear, but eventually I felt the surface beneath the tires changing from ice to water.

Just outside the park, I pulled into a restaurant, a timber frame building that usually offered a wide view of the Front Range. In the bar, a fire was roaring in the big stone fireplace. I walked to a stool, propped my elbows on the shiny wooden surface before me, and slid my hands inside my sweater sleeves, seeking warmth just as I had earlier, beneath the tree. My skin was still cold to the touch.

The bartender walked toward me, gesturing at my wet hair. "Got caught in the weather, huh?"

"I did."

He gestured toward the window. "Well it's sure socked-in up there. Gonna snow a little here tonight, they say."

I ordered coffee with a shot of Irish whiskey. It went down hot and began to spread through me, into my arms and legs, my fingers. False warmth, I knew. But it felt good.

The view of the Front Range had not changed since I'd sat in the parking lot: the Rockies were still hidden in that eerie thick nothingness. Safe inside and warming, I made myself think about what could have happened up there. I knew the risks. One careless step, a long cold slide off the trail. Broken bones, concussion. And no one to miss me for a long time.

But I hadn't been afraid. Instead, I had felt the weight of my responsibility for myself. To use my knowledge and my common sense to make it out by placing one foot carefully in front of the other. My task didn't change when Ben appeared: the only thing I could do for him was to be very careful with myself.

The bartender offered me more coffee and I took it, holding the hot cup gratefully in my hands, sitting on, alone in the bar as he went back to work polishing glasses.

*

Snow fell on Estes Park that night. I lay on the couch near the fire wondering how I would make myself leave this place tomorrow. How long would it be until I had a day like this all to myself, a day, whatever it brought, to replenish the resources that sustain me, day to day, year by year? Just then the phone rang, and I heard my daughters' voices.

"Did you have fun today, Mom?"

"When will you be here?" We found a tarantula in the garage."

What is it that flight attendants tell us about the oxygen masks that drop down from the ceilings of airplanes? Against all our best instincts, they caution, we must put our own masks on first, and then assist others with theirs. Parenting is more complicated than that, but the principle applies. Heading up the mountain alone, late in the day, might have been foolhardy-my father would have said so. But it was also an act of preservation. Save yourself first, then look to the children.

When the conversation ran down, I walked outside. Snow glistened in the light from the windows, but out there across the valley, the mountains remained hidden.

Pamela Gibbs Hirschler
Ironworker Choreography

Inside the chain link fence, the worker crouches
on the beam, throws a line around the post,
stands and walks with heel-toe steps—a careful,
slow ballet. He waves a hand—a signal
to the crane—guides the steel into the plate,
aligns the holes, inserts the ready bolt,
then sits and calmly slides along the beam,
looks up and grabs the line, unsnaps the hook.
The welder rises slowly from below.
He leans against the rails with steady hands,
welds the joint, then clears away the slag,
grinds the weld bead down in showered sparks
until the steel is smooth. Outside the fence,
the homeless chain their carts and watch the light.

Dorothy Hopkins Schnare
Star Bred

Burn orange rind as innocent incense.
Ignore temperate urges; explore much.
Push upriver, shiver but find silence.
Miracle of mindfulness prompts a hunch.

Touch rainbow waters chasing theorems.
Embrace miracles with fond attention.
Presence not mind games translates requiems.
Awareness awakens brash intuition.

Brush the edge. If your practice is landing
In the moment, you will find that the work
Of breath prompts the heart as the bush standing
Winter lets the lilac sprig near the church.

Just as stars solicit our sharp seeing,
Transport us from nothingness to being.

Second Place 2018 Joy Bale Boone Poetry Prize

Elaine Fowler Palencia
The Buttonhook

I want a tarnished silver buttonhook
that can pick the locked gate
to an old frame house
standing in a yard
full of heirloom flowers
found in no catalogue today
in a valley left off the map.

Inside the house, I want to find
a library of leather-bound books
whose authors died before writing them,
and a musty piano with outlawed ivory keys,
its bench full of nocturnes
their composers forgot to write down.

I want to find a penciled note
under a loose tile in the fireplace
My name is William
I am twelve years old
It is the year 1893
I am so unhappy
Will you write to me?

I want to write William
at a desk lit by wax tapers burning down
like young girls blazing with tuberculosis
as I sit next to a hulking pendulum clock
that reels time backwards
so that in the tick and tock
of our correspondence,
William and I can figure out
how to save all who got lost
trying to find the road
out of the past.

Richard Foerster
The Falling Rocket

Detroit Institute of Arts

does not look like a rocket; it imprints
the night blue, yellow, green with soundless
dazzle, turmoil's smoke and fog, sensation
with no hint of moral in the aftermath of chaos.

Two women stand at the water's edge, transparent
as tea, pure vessels of the intangible moment
there in the distance. Luminous ambiguity
passes through them, intimate as danger or delight.

Ruskin accused Whistler with having flung a pot
of paint in the public's face, a libel worth then,
as now, a farthing. Have we been schooled
in failed aesthetics? Here, children with Crayolas

litter the halls, sketching what they've been told
to see; their teacher hovers, beams, then pauses
above one rapt in peculiar dark, one whose fingers
sputter like a fuse, intent on detonation.

Richard Taylor
Chickadee

Reading in my armchair
by the window this winter morning,
my eye catches peripheral motion: a
black-capped chickadee, inches
away on the cold side of the glass.

What I want to write about
is not the crook of its legs
that bend like bobby pins,
the tiny claws defying gravity
to clamp the bar of the muntin.

No, nor the tufts of feathers
as colorless as dust
or that nervous pertness in the eye.
What I want to put down on paper is
not the bird itself
but the space from which
it has just flown.

E. Gail Chandler
Even the Carpenter has Left Town

We walk by the walrus,
his turbulent tail vexed
and thwacking.

Our eyelets meet his peepers.
He does not yarn on cabbages,
for his kingdom is a-molder,

his palace filled with nurdles,
his ocean all asunder.
The oysters have liquidated

and his breadbasket's been forsaken.
We cast our eyelets downward,
and fluidly schlep away.

Honorable Mention 2018 Joy Bale Boone Poetry Prize

Jill Bergkamp
Bird, How like a Magician

We'll plant a garden labyrinth, boil starfruit into jam,
rebuild the hot house, and foster children.
We whispered like teens at sleepaway camp

in our striped hammock, about the bees we'd tend together,
the worms wriggling in compost from our banana peels
and coffee grounds; the small tines of raccoon prints

we'd find in the mornings,
and the red eared sliders scrabbling through bushes
like little drunks.

If the peacock ever leaves, I'll kidnap you a new one, you promised,
while every night it cobbled past us and circled the live oak
until, neck tensed, it flew to the tree's lowest branch.

We tangled arms and legs and slapped at mosquitos
as the bird navigated, hopping till it reached the highest branch.
And when we turned away we couldn't locate

its shape in the dark. We fell in love
with our dreams of ourselves and the bird
with that marvelous disappearing.

Michele Parker Randall
Dropping a Tree

To kill a tree, you ring it,
cut bark back so the water
can't flow. The tree closest
to the house has been peeled
and drained. The man who comes
to drop the tree between houses
considers other angles, looks
at the tree, walks full around,
touches the bark, and sits at its feet,
before he ever makes the first cut.
When chainsaw bites tree flesh,
he stops every few inches, drives
a shim deep in with a hammer.
And with a swing, not the chain,
the tree begins to fall, and fall straight,
and I know: this is not his first tree,
this is how I should approach all things.

Norma Calway-Fagen
The Least Worse Person

You read it anyway because she asked. At least that's what you tell yourself after. But face it: the truth is you couldn't man-up enough to say no. It's not the end of the world. After all, you two are in a downswing. Distant. You in front of the computer. Her somewhere you aren't. Weeks have gone by without either of you asking anything more personal than how was your day.

It doesn't matter that the night before last, for the first time in forever, you had sex. Good toe-curling sex that left you panting for your next breath. Two near strangers, excitement fed by a sense of anonymity.

So you said yes. Even though you knew you weren't going to like it. It was her voice. The challenging tone. That was all you needed to hear. The article is downloaded to her iPhone, probably from the New Yorker or the New York Times. Somewhere totally unrelated to the way most of the world lives its life. It says something about how people need to do away with the romantic notion of love. That it causes them to marry the wrong person. Not on purpose. But because the wrong person is familiar. Or at least the feelings you and the wrong person create are familiar. Feelings from childhood, what you grew up with. They feel safe because you know them.

She watches for your reaction. You look around the dining room. The report you are working on is scattered across the glass-top table. What a crock, you think. You remember the silence of your parents whenever they were in a room together. Or late at night when your mother took long walks after an argument. You were terrified that she wasn't coming back. Until one day she didn't. Now you're being told you want to feel like that same scared little boy peering anxiously out the door counting the minutes. You stare at Olivia.

"You've got to be kidding me."

"Don't get mad before you even finish the article."

So you read on. The good news is that if you played it right, didn't get caught up in romance, you could end up with the least worse person and have a chance for a good marriage. So that's it, you think. The best you can hope for is to marry the person who is least wrong for you.

"Is that what I am to you?" You hate the hurt in your voice. So you get mad. "We don't live in New fucking York. We're not cynics. This isn't cool, Olivia."

"Come on, Brian. Don't get on your soapbox. I just wondered what you thought."

What you think at the moment is that last night, you had sex. She even let you enter her from behind. That takes trust, doesn't it? But when you remind her of that, she laughs.

"That's sex, not love. Good sex, for sure, and not something I would do with just anybody. But still not love." She looks directly at you. "This isn't a comment about us. I just thought it was an interesting way to look at relationships."

"Don't bullshit me," you say, glaring. You try to control yourself but you can't stop the fear spreading through your chest. She tells you she is going to bed. The conversation, as she puts it, is going nowhere.

You leave your house the next morning. Neighbors are still asleep in their darkened houses. A glimmer of light pokes through the dark. At work, you finish the report. The one you got sidetracked from the night before. Later, you sit in your car outside your office, sip a cup of coffee, and think, what a lousy night. The argument. No sleep. You feel and look like crap. So had Olivia, you were relieved to see, before you left home. But she was like ice. Barely a hello exchanged. As you pull out of the driveway at work, you wonder where the hell she gets off being mad at you. You swear you won't let it bother you. But it does. Love does that to you.

Mrs. Crockett, a skinny woman with greying hair, waits in her front yard. No introductions necessary. She was your sixth-grade science teacher. Of course, she agreed to participate in your study. Not surprising really. Truth is, things came pretty easy to you back then. Grades. Team captain. Dates every weekend. Sometimes you wondered if it was because of your mother. That part hadn't been easy. Anything but. You quickly quell that thought.

After all, Mrs. Crockett told you the day you had asked her to participate, "Maybe you'll cite me as an early influence. Marine biologist inspired by grade school teacher. Something like that." You just smiled. She has a stake in your success—her star pupil, sure, but it is also her land that first showed the effects of the sea's encroachment.

She tells you to follow her around back where her yard and land, a couple of acres, fronts the Bay. The land is squishy under your feet. It doesn't even look like a yard anymore. More like a Florida marsh.

"Look at this." She pushes the toe of her canvas shoe into the ground. Water pools. "It stays wet all the time now. Doesn't dry out."

You find another spot, press down, and watch water seep up from the earth. You do a slow 180. See the clumps of cordgrass. The leaves matted together by salt from sea spray and frequent gale-force winds. You look out beyond the grass to the bay. Battered fishing boats dot the horizon. Crouching down, you stare at hundreds of holes filled with water.

"Fiddler crabs." Mrs. Crockett nods in acknowledgement.

As a child, your mother would say, "Look, Brian," and point to the fiddler crabs scurrying along the beach. Their color changed with the ebb and flow of the tides, she told you. Dark during the day, light at night. You ran up and down the beach laughing as you chased the crabs. She laughed with you. And told you about an oyster midden that lies just off shore. Made it seem like something ancient, mysterious. You felt lucky to live in such a magical place. It was this, the magic of the sea and the laughter in your mother's voice that led you to marine biology.

Now with the ocean surge, the midden is several miles further out, the island of your childhood is disappearing, and your mother is gone. And then there's last night. You'd thought you were finished with loneliness. You take some measurements and look over at Mrs. Crockett. She knows from your expression. Had known before she'd even called you. Her brown eyes moisten, "It's bad isn't it, Brian? Goddammit." She stares out at the water while you tell her the bay has advanced another ten feet. Grain by grain, her yard and the island are being consumed by the rising sea.

You have lunch with Vivianne, your ex-girlfriend. She looks good. Dark hair cut short on one side, shoulder length on the other. Contrasted by intense blue eyes. The hair suits her. For a minute, you let your mind go somewhere it shouldn't.

She's a conceptual artist. A "liver of life" as her website says. You talk about a collaborative project. About the environment, the warming of the oceans. What's happening here and elsewhere. No one paying attention. Your talk moves on to mutual friends who have left the island. One is landlocked somewhere in Kentucky as far from the water and rising seas as she can get. The other started a bakery in Seattle. She does bake cakes for gays. You pretend to be interested, but your mind is elsewhere.

You met Olivia just after you and Vivianne broke up. You two were practically married, except for a few undisclosed occasions when you were, let's be real, less than faithful. More honest, Vivianne didn't really care. Hell, she barely had time for you between her part-time job and full-time dedication to her art. Which was why, you liked to tell yourself, you found yourself between the legs of that redhead. Vivianne, meanwhile, had found her own blond version of your redhead, a looker and an artist like she was.

One morning you heard Vivianne crying. You found her in the kitchen, shuffling from refrigerator to stove, making her breakfast. Her nose red, she was still snuffling when you entered the room.

Uh oh, you thought. You put your arms around her and pulled her to you.

"What's wrong, babe?"

She put her head on your shoulder and cried some more. And that is how you ended up hugging her when she told you she didn't love you. No, that's not exactly it. She told you she loved you but she wasn't in love with you. You failed to see the distinction.

"Not in the way I feel about Lenna. I'm so sorry, Brian. I never meant to hurt you."

You told yourself it didn't matter. The woman's gay, right? Nothing against you. You knew something was off. No wonder you made it with other women.

But all that was a long time ago. Now you are friends. Almost best friends, so you decide to tell her about last night. It was like a hit and run you say. First, she slammed you with the article. Least worse person—can you believe that shit? And then acted like there was something wrong with you. "What a bitch," you say. Maybe, you tell your ex, if you'd just read it. Not said anything.

Vivianne never liked Olivia. A Virgo. Wrong from the beginning as she'd told you.

"Virgo's are linear, Bri, and you're the least linear scientist I know. It won't work."

There'd been no point in reminding her that you and she had been astrologically compatible, and look where that got you.

"What do you think? "A mistake—you know it as soon as you ask. The way she stares at you. Waiting, as if reluctant to let loose. But once she starts. Well no need for all the details.

"Brian…" A big pause—you're in for it now. "You're such a fucking romantic."

You know where she's going but can't stop yourself. "And what's wrong with that?"

"Well, for one thing, you only see what you want to see. Total denial. Makes it hard to tell you things. Look at us."

Now she's to it. What she wanted to say from the beginning. You ask what the hell that has to do with Olivia. Whose side is she on anyway?

"OK Brian. You're right. I'm sorry. I just hate to see you hurt."

Later, you realize Vivianne was right about one thing—the part about Olivia being a Virgo. But that was about it you decide. Hell, what about the night you met Olivia. Nothing linear about that. You'd been through the after break-up, frantic hook-ups. Flipped through enough pictures on Tinder and collected enough phone numbers to keep ahead of the itch and reassure yourself that you still had it. So when Kevin first mentioned the club, you'd told him no way. But Kevin being Kevin, not to mention your best friend since grade school—you end up going. Five hours later, you're slightly drunk and mad at yourself for having said yes. Then you see her. It's not her looks, although she's pretty enough. But not the prettiest. Slender without being thin. Dark hair pulled back from her face. All good but not what caused you to stare. It was the way she carried herself. Self-possessed but not in an I'm hot shit way. Natural. You felt a powerful wave of desire as she walked your way. "I want to kiss you," she said.

Falling asleep that night, you were happier than you've been in some time. Olivia, you thought. Now that's a name to hold onto. Of course, as it turned out, there were differences. She liked non-fiction. You read everything and anything. She didn't like bugs or dirt. You wanted to hike the Appalachian Trail. She wasn't much for music. You're a lapsed

Methodist. She's Jewish. Had grown up in New York City, Columbia Law School. The whole northeast big-city scene. But it had worked. Love conquers all, right?

*T*hat night you and Olivia are carefully careless—choosing your words but trying not to seem like you are. At least you're talking. Sort of.

She tells you about a case she is working on, and you act interested. You tell her about Mrs. Crockett and the swamp. What that means for the island but also for the two of you. You've talked about moving. Probably should have moved when you could have. Now real estate prices are down. Besides, who are you fooling? You love it here—love that there are few cars and one traffic light. Love that Kevin your best friend from first grade still lives here. You tell her about lunch with Vivianne. Yes, she does look great, you say. Seems happy with Lenna. What you don't tell her is what Vivianne said, the stuff about you being a romantic. Eventually you get around to the previous night's argument.

"Why did you get so mad?" she asks.

You try to explain, but you're not really sure yourself. "You're saying us, our relationship, isn't love—"

"That's not what I said. I just asked you to read an article. That's all. But, Brian, what if sometimes what is important to me is different than what is important to you? I can't be worried about your feelings all the time. I have to be able to tell you what I think, or it won't work."

That's not the only thing that might not work, you want to say. But instead you tell her she's trying to make it your fault.

"Everything isn't about fault, Brian. I just wonder why you want me to use your words. Why the hell you can't accept what I say, the way I say it? I feel like your pressuring me."

"What do you mean?"

"It seems like you want me to prove that I care about you. But nothing ever seems enough."

"That's bullshit. You showed me the article, remember. How's that putting pressure on you. It might be different if things were better between us. So excuse me if I wonder what you're trying to tell me? What's your point?"

"Don't be stupid, Brian. There was no point," she tells you. But her words have nothing to do with love. Not once have you said you love me, you want to shout. Marrying someone because they are not as bad as someone else—or a little better than someone—that's not why you married her. So what if you're a romantic?

The thaw has frozen over and you're back to where you were. Another bedtime without even a good-night. Part of you wants to bury your face between Olivia's soft breasts. But that's not happening. Not when she clutches a pillow tight to her body, as clear as a keep-off sign. You think back to the beginning. Was it possible this had never come up?

You make it through the next couple of days. Push paper around on your desk. Try to look productive but not really fooling anyone. You reschedule a couple of meetings with the excuse that you need a day or two more to finalize your results. Instead, you drop in on colleagues, one cubicle at a time. You skip Mr. Hays. He's too old to understand, and John Mackle, whose just an asshole. You've practiced your approach. Just checking in you start—wait a few minutes—give them a chance to talk. Pretend you're listening. Then, and this is where you know you have to be careful, keep it casual. Not like you care or anything.

"Hey, just read this article," you show her the title, "and wondering what you think?"

"New Yorker, right?" Katherine asks. You nod yes. "Should have known," she says. "Romance is out, Brian. We're not cool anymore. Not this decade anyway."

"Yeah, that's just what my wife said." A lie maybe. But necessary.

You feel vindicated, armed and ready for Olivia. Until you meet Kevin for a run that afternoon. He sees right through the lie. "Dude, get over it. Grow a pair."

Later, you tell Olivia what Katherine said. She laughs. "That's the one who wears her hair like Alice in Wonderland, raved about The Notebook right?" Not exactly the response you want. Maybe that's why you go on to tell her Kevin's comment.

She looks at you like you are a ground-crawling life form. "Dude? Who the hell says dude at 31? Come on, Bri, or should I say bro? You can do better than that."

The clarity of her coldness surprises you. "And you're not the person I met three years ago."

Next day you drive past your old house and stop. It looks pretty much the same—painted white with a front porch that runs the length of the house. The red maple, a little taller now, still grows by your old bedroom window. And the creek, you and Kevin waded in, skirts the back of the property. But anger prickles when you notice your mother's irises gone. Even the rare bearded variety had been pulled up, replaced by what looks like low-maintenance bushes. In your mind, you see your mother, straw hat on head, barefoot and seated between the irises, dividing and transplanting bulbs. She's been dead for years now. Kissed you good-bye one morning and was gone by the afternoon. Anger grips you. What had started as an argument had come to be everything else. Your mother's death, the island disappearing, and now this thing with Olivia.

You make it to Mrs. Crockett's, barely. Distracted, you drive by her house. Mrs. Crockett waves as you go by.

"Forget where you're going?' She laughs when you get out of your car. You feel terrible. You want to care about Mrs. Crockett, the island, your study. But the anger won't leave you.

"Are you OK?" Concern creases her face.

"I don't want to talk about it." You say, and then tell yourself that Mrs. Crockett deserves better than that.

"Sorry, just a rough day. I'm fine, really." Except you're not. You know it and she knows it.

She moves closer, grips your arm. "You going to tell me what's wrong?"

You shake your head and look out to the bay. The boats are coming in trailed by screeching seagulls anxious to share in the day's catch. It must be later than you think. You turn your face to hers, meet her eyes.

"Everything's shit, if you really want to know. The island's dying, no-one cares but us, and…" You take a deep breath. When you feel like you can go on without anger, you say, "And my wife doesn't love me."

Mrs. Crockett sighs and pulls her sweater around her. The wind has picked up, threatening to bring rain with it. After several seconds she says, "Is that what she told you? Those words?"

You look at her. You've never noticed how small she was. Not a pretty woman, putty-like nose and thin lips. But her deep brown eyes are comforting.

She's the one you tell. About the article and the argument—that when you thought it might get better it hadn't. About how sad you are. About the fear too. You can't shake it. You failed your mother. And she died. But most of all the marrow-deep feeling of anger. Your mother didn't die, not down there in all the rage. She left you when you most needed her. Now this. You take a long time to get it all out. But it helps. She talks about her life. Things you never knew. Her marriage. How love, real love is work. It's hard, takes courage. But also needs the belief in possibilities to grow. She taps you on the chest over your heart. "Listen to this," she says. "It's a good one. It's up to you to know how much you want to handle." Mrs. Crockett opens her arms, pulls you into them. You lay your head against her chest. It is bony, not much there, but it is good. It is her words, her soft voice and the way she holds you. You feel safe.

You get home early, surprised to see Olivia there on the couch waiting. "I'm glad your home, Brian. I've been sitting here wondering what we're fighting about." she says, patting the couch. "Let's talk."

Her face is mottled from crying. Part of you wants to go to her, but you need more time. You think about the past few days, the article, and the time before that, when things had gotten bad. What did either of you know about love? You think about your mother, the two of you running up and down the beach, laughing. You think about Mrs. Crockett, what she said about love and listening to yourself and being listened to. You realize the hard part is just beginning, and you're not sure where it will lead. Sighing, you shake your head. "Not now, Olivia. I need more time. We'll talk tomorrow." You touch her shoulder to show you're not mad.

Honorable Mention 2018 Joy Bale Boone Poetry Prize

George Drew
After Your Reading in the Adirondacks

--To Michael Meyerhofer

After your reading in the Adirondacks
there I was, tooling along on Interstate 87
south toward Uncle Sam's hometown,
and I got to thinking wouldn't it be

a piss if out of nowhere some idiot
going north in a southbound lane
ran into me headfirst at forty miles
per hour above the limit; or maybe

an 18-wheeler rammed me from behind,
or from the back of an open-bed truck
thirty Porta-Potties tumbled ass
over end and clobbered me, or a poodle

loose in a pickup got bounced out
and shattered my windshield and me—
I can just see the headline: POET KILLED
BY PINK POODLE. Great. But of course

none of these happened and I got home
still totally hungover from your poetry
and thinking: Man, I'm glad I'm not
James Dean tearing up that California road

in his silver Porsche 550 Spyder bomb;
glad I'm not Albert Camus wrapping his
Facel Vega HK500 around that tree
so goddamned randomly one afternoon;

glad I'm not Jackson Pollock the night
he lost his head, his blue Olds 88
flipping the world the bird; glad even
I'm not Hank Williams the night

his heart went flat in the back seat
of that blue '52 Caddy. Bette Davis was
right when she said old age ain't
for sissies, but neither is being young.

I'm glad you're only thirty-five and still
trucking, your foot free of lead, your brain
cruising the neighborhood, and Bette's dictum
aside, glad too I've been here twice as long.

Hannah Pelletier
A Houseguest Named Joy

I never even told it where I lived—
certainly

did not
invite
it

to stay with me, but
there it came

stomping through the
house with

shoeless feet,

rewriting every book
in the house

until they were
all backwards,

even my
poems

turned the wrong
shade. Without hands,

it locked
the door to

my
favorite room I

could not
get over

the grief

of all the loves
it demanded I

let go of.

After kicking it
to the curb

it stayed

watching outside
my window nearly

three days

but when it was
gone,

it was gone & left
nothing

behind itself.

Third Place 2018 Joy Bale Boone Poetry Prize

Maggie Blake Bailey
A Flood Like That Would Be Better

By the road, hunched like old women,
a cluster of birds, heavy shouldered
and menacing. Surely the dark
shine of their bodies means buzzards,
means death or something similar.

They stand, sliced into the red
of cranberry bog and I think
about drowning, or floating
like those sharp-tasting berries,
drifting up and free for the harvest.

I think a flood like that would be better
than this drive to my mother's house.
I want the water to rise slowly, to rise
kindly, the way they say you can boil
lobsters by slowly turning up the heat.

They won't even notice. I wish
the heavy bodied birds are osprey,
taloned fish hawks drifted inland,
ready to swoop, not buzzards waiting
to find what has already died.

They will be here tomorrow:
the bog, the birds, the low
stone walls of an old town.
Carrion birds and the long
drive to my mother's house.

Jessica Walsh
Nails Done

Above the line is the time before

Rhinestones once
a skull on my middle finger
because fuck the world I'd say
before it fucked me up

I say money but it's not
Truth is I don't know her
the one with pretty useless claws

Today I am the woman who
wakes up worried about mice
and crawls the floor with a flashlight

thinks of making muffins but doesn't
because who knows what we eat now

hopes for no calls

studies your neck for swelling
and tries to pass off the stares as love

All this grows out they tell me
and my hands will look just like they used to

James Trask
Green is the Cradle

Green is the cradle, rocking me to sleep;
I seek a covered or uncovered bed,
Where ancient whispers soothe with cooling heat.

Brown the headboard, cracked with rivers deep,
Splendid towers to conquered lands be wed;
Green is the cradle, rocking me to sleep.

Green is the blanket reaching from beneath,
A polymelia thousand-legged arachnid
Cushions me with fingers of cooling heat.

Orange are these walls that cannot be seen,
Unless you search with thrice-blessed eyes of the dead;
Green is the cradle, rocking me to sleep.

Hums of a hundred voices at once all speak,
Close beside; I strain to taste, instead,
Ancient whispers like drops of cooling heat.

Covert lead-lined strings untie from me;
I am no longer someone's marionette;
Green is the cradle, rocking me to sleep,
Where ancient whispers soothe with cooling heat.

Margaret Koger
Ripe Figs

A Franco-Catalan artist's
Le Musèe Maillol displays
nouveau tapestries of women
who lean into trees, pillars, beds
nude curves you've seen
in mind and mirror.

Maillol's ripest fascinations
spent on classic curves
robust bronze bodies
of women sculpted to lean
on trees, pillars, beds
their lips slightly uplifted.

Imagine a girl demeaned
by her shoddy round-tummy.
Maillol restores her dignity
his oil paintings of auras
swearing to nubile summers.

Here on her bedroom wall
hang up his woodblock print
a woman, neither fat nor thin
paired with a study of red figs.

Minney Richani
Hob Wa Harb

Lebanon 1920's spared the roof over our heads
And lovers left their mark in smears of lust
Decorating the fragile walls with honesty
Our ancestors wasted their courage on wars
So instead we fight to claim each other's hearts
Encouraging me to the heights of Aley's mountains
So that I fall for you at the magnitude of altitudes
And the moments our lips let generosity slip
Your unguarded eyes spill promises
And my skin beneath your unsettled breath
Contrasts with the rough wall against my back
And yet they are the same
Stories of history in the folds of our future
And my voice only ineligible whispers
And yet your hands respond by touching my soul
And my tongue is cocoa sweetened by your accent
With bitterness only tracing the word we don't want to hear
In a place that hadn't been given the chance for any last words
In a place that will remember our pounding hearts
Forgetting our unbalanced footsteps in the ruble ground
The way the Middle East went out of focus
As it framed you in the centre of my being

Younger Artists

Amna Ahmed
Unbridled Spirit

Kin in a land called 'Tucky.
Whispered promises of soft spoken hills
agitated by Irish air.

Its bourbon secrets pleated
in grassy knolls who pluck
their bluegrass fiddles of sun shined pastures.

Your stable is my refuge,
your river my blazed discord.
Sleepless slumbers in the heartland.
Unsettled, unfiltered, unbridled spirit.

Divya Chhotani
Laughing Crime

When one is down in the dump,
We sing a happy song
Of tales of dragons with its eyes cut off
And emblazing us with flames from above.
We hear of knights in shining armor
of memories that we have forgot,
Running through time in a magic carpet
Like Aladdin on drugs.

When we laugh and play all day,
The crime is already done.
We hide our faces from the dangers …
Which is indeed our mum.
We jump and play and be rambunctious,
We sing too many songs,
Laughing and crying and being dizzy
Is the name of the song I love.

The crime the crime the wonderful crime
Of selfish pigeons and ugly rhymes,
The song skips one not two but three
Beats at one time,
Beating like a heart about to explode,
Cardiac arrest I'm told.
I am lucky that I am alive singing the song of love,
Jumping and giggling, my stomach is jiggling,
I can feel my body erupt.

The laugh and crime I do till I
Fall over and die.
The stage of life, a rhythm of life,
The continuous stages of grief,
In heaven I play I jump all day,
I never will run away.

Esha Nattu
HOME:

What is a home?
Something that never goes away.
But it's not a fire, not a bed,
not soup.

It's love- in many different forms.
It's love that seeps and weeps-
Lives in your blood.

But why should the heart pump such blood?
For the joy of reminiscence, too seek comfort
When you're lost.

Like a bacterium, it doubles and doubles
And doubles. Like a fungus it rots and rots,
Until the feeling is revived again.
Fresh as a waterfall, strong like an ocean.

HOME. The sonorous sound heals.
Louder than a clap of thunder,
Louder than a gunshot,
The sound heals.

HOME.
It can never be erased from my memory
And that's what's so beautiful about it.

Kendall Vanderwouw
Winter Remembrance

White flakes of wonder coat the ground with beauty.
Their echoing curiosity inflicts its magical essence
upon my mind.
The floating clouds allow their flourishing essence
to flutter from the pale sky,
almost the golden, glowing light of a miracle.
Winter calls upon these wonders to represent in our mind
a sign of magic.
Proving once again that nature truly is a force of power,
always guiding the wizardry of winter.
The fields of white frost glowing in our once-forgotten
winter light seem to appear
as if a conjured, fictitious moment
of my romanticizing imagination.
Their luminous calling enchanting me, like a lion with deceit,
lurking deep into my memories, yet allowing me to rediscover
my childish imagination.
The flakes of snow become fairies
leading me down the footsteps I took in my childhood adventures.
Winter playing upon my fond memories,
as I salvage the sentimental moments forgotten
that are tied to these poised memories.
Fading agony coats my mind
when these moments seem to slip from my grasp of memory,
no matter how dearly I hold them,
like a dragon guarding treasure.
The true mistress winter the only thing
that allows my sensations to reappear.
For winter truly sentimentalizes the hope
we hold in our aching hearts.

Lacey Trautwein
They Say

They Say

this is quite common
reaction to losing
one's innocence--
forcibly.

Genitalia is as common as
a pizza parlor:
What toppings will you have today, young lady?
enunciating young and lady as
if he's sizing me up--
the slicer begins to
saw the labia off.
My meal.

Their Pepsi machine is strictly for consuming
a suicide churning
one's stomach--
purposely.

The cashier smirks with the hint of metal wafting
from his crooked teeth,
sharp daggers to my buds,
tasting it with every inhale,
with every bite.

Out of my bones pours Sex
Ed. pamphlets,
Like, no please don't,
knobby knees shake and are pink with
shame swirl
with trifecta blood watercolor drops
of his essence.

Gracie Yates
Unspoken Battles

Your face
Changes, it turns sour
It's bitter
Just like the words on my tongue
I regret them
As soon as they fall from my lips
The blush
As if I had marked you a rose myself
The intake of air
My words take your breath away
A blow to the chest leaves you aching
Tongue like a dagger
Words like knives
I've got a vocabulary of soldiers
Lined up to fight the battles
I never should have chosen

Cheyenne Koth
Love Poem
to the southern fisherwoman

She knows the banks, how fish hide,
She knows to move slow,
achingly slow, so as not to startle
Her shimmering prey.

She wades through the shallows,
taro leaves brushing
the tree trunks of Her calves.

Gazing over leaf-browned water,
muscled cords of Her biceps poised
for the quick finality— the swish.

Contributor Notes

As a senior at Elizabethtown High School in Kentucky, **Amna Ahmed** plans to attend Indiana University to study International Relations. As an alumna of the Kentucky Governor's School for the Arts Creative Writing Program, Amna uses "poetry to express my identity as a young multicultural American living in Kentucky."

Jill Bergkamp teaches at Palm Beach Atlantic University, and has poems published in *Sugarhouse Review, Rattle, Gargoyle*, and *Image*. She was the recipient of the Rona Jaffe Foundation Broadleaf Poetry Scholarship in 2008, and an Image Glen Workshop poetry scholarship in 2013.

Maggie Blake Bailey has poems published or forthcoming in *The San Pedro River Review, Tar River, Ruminate*, and elsewhere. Her chapbook *Bury the Lede* is available from Finishing Line Press and her full length debut *Visitation* (Tinderbox Editions) will be available in 2019. For more work, please visit www.maggieblakebailey.com.

E. Gail Chandler is an Appalachian, a Vietnam veteran, and is retired from Kentucky Corrections. Finishing Line has published two of her poetry chapbooks: *Where the Red Road Meets the Sky* (2003) and *He Read to Us* (2016).

Divya Chhotani is a student at Westwood High School in Austin, Texas.

George Drew is the author of seven poetry collections, most recently *Pastoral Habits: New and Selected Poems, Down & Dirty* and *The View From Jackass Hill*, winner of the 2010 X.J. Kennedy Poetry Prize, all from Texas Review Press. His eighth, *Fancy's Orphan*, appeared in 2017, Tiger Bark Press.

Norma Calway-Fagen lives in Nashville where she has worked as a clinical psychologist for many years. In the past two years, she has committed more time to writing, including completing an MFA in Creative Writing at Murray State University.

Richard Foerster is the author of seven poetry collections: *Sudden Harbor* and *Patterns of Descent* (Orchises Press), *Trillium, Double Going*, and *The Burning of Troy* (BOA Editions), and *Penetralia* and *River Road* (Texas Review Press). *Boy on a Doorstep: New and Selected Poems* is forthcoming from Tiger Bark Press in Spring 2019.

Pamela Gibbs Hirschler is a native Kentuckian whose poetry has appeared in *Still: The Journal, The Heartland Review, Pine Mountain Sand & Gravel*, and is forthcoming in *Talking River*. She holds an MFA in Poetry from Drew University.

Janice Fuller is a speech pathologist turned poet who lives in Arizona and Wisconsin. She says "Inspiration for my poems often comes from my life in these two very different places." Fuller's other work can be seen in *Desert Voices* and *From the Depths.*

Jo Friel is the 2018 Central Kentucky Art Guild Artist of the Year.

Margaret Koger is a school-media specialist. She lives and works in Boise, Idaho and celebrates le bois--the trees the city is named for. She's published most recently in *Poetry Breakfast, Mediterranean Poetry, Anthology Askew: Love Gone Askew and Mused.*

Melissa Hassard was awarded the 2016 Thomas H. McDill Award, placed as a finalist for the 2016 North Carolina Poet Laureate Award, and received Honorable Mention in the 2014 Randall Jarrell Poetry Award. A Pushcart Prize nominee, Hassard's poems have appeared in a number of journals. She is partner and managing editor at Sable Books where she co-edited *RED SKY*, an anthology of poetry on the global epidemic of violence against women.

From Charleston, South Carolina, **Cheyenne Koth** is currently attending Flagler College in hopes of one day becoming a park ranger. Cheyenne enjoys learning about the past, drawing, and writing poems. They will soon be published in the anthology *Third Wednesday*, and has one book of poems published, titled *History, Love, and Other Things I'm Not Making*.

Kevin J. McDaniel lives in Pulaski, VA with his wife, two daughters, and their menagerie of pets. His work can be found in the *Anthology of Appalachian Writers: Wiley Cash Volume X, Artemis Journal*, and *Broad River Review*, among others. His recent chapbook, *Family Talks*, was published by Finishing Line Press in 2017.

Esha Natu, a sophomore at Monta Vista High School, lives in Cupertino, California. Esha says "I'm a dreamer. I dream of doing many things to make the world a better place. I'm all about being a part of the change. In school, I like studying all the natural sciences and English. I have a passion for poetry."

Elaine Fowler Palencia, Champaign IL, is the author of two short story collection, three poetry chapbooks, and a scholarly monograph, The Literary Heritage of Hindman Settlement School (2017). Her work has received seven Pushcart Prize nominations.

Hannah Pelletier studied English at the University of New Hampshire where she received the prestigious Richard M. Ford writing award two years in a row. Hannah is an expat currently living in Nancy, France with her husband and fifteen fish.

Michele Parker Randall authored *Museum of Everyday Life* (Kelsay Books), and her work has appeared in various literary publications. She was a finalist for the Peter Meinke Poetry Prize and the 2017 Beulah Rose Poetry Prize.

Minney Richani likes to drink coffee, make deplorable mistakes she doesn't regret and write. Her writing is influenced by past and current relationships, her clashing Australian/Syrian nationality, her strong views towards any form of discrimination and the constant struggle of finding herself.

Born in Berlin, New Hampshire, **Dorothy Hopkins Schnare** ended up in Kentucky via New Orleans, Florida and Saudi Arabia. She is a steady, unprolific poet. Recent publication includes an anthology with four other Berea poets entitled: *Balance of Five*, Foreword by bell hooks.

Heidi Seaborn starting writing poetry in 2016. Her work appears in over 50 journals and anthologies. Heidi's chapbook, *Finding My Way Home*, is published by Finishing Line Press in March 2018.

Richard Taylor was Kentucky Poet Laureate of the Commonwealth of Kentucky from 1999-2001. Taylor is the author of six collections of poetry, two historical novels, and several works of nonfiction and history. His most recent book is *Rail Splitter*, a collection of poems based on Lincoln's life, published by Larkspur Press. Taylor has won two creative writing fellowships from the National Endowment for the Arts. He is an antiquarian book dealer.

James Trask lives in New Jersey and works in Manhattan with an investment team. He is a US Army veteran. He has published poems with Jersey City Writers and the Mountain Journal, and is currently finishing his first full length poetry manuscript.

Lacey Trautwein is a poet living in Frankfort, KY with her cat, Stanley. She reads *Poetry for Gigantic Sequins.* Her poetry has been featured in *The Kentucky River.* She recently won a fellowship to SAFTA's writing retreat for sexual assault survivors. She is at work on her first chapbook.

Kendall Vanderwouw is an middle-school student from Nevada City, California. She began writing at age seven, when she started using poetry to express her views. Writing has become her outlet to cope with hardships, express joy, and share her passions.

Jessica L. Walsh is the author of the poetry collection *How to Break My Neck* as well as two chapbooks. Her work has appeared or is forthcoming in *RHINO, Tinderbox, White Stag, Whale Road, Midwestern Gothic*, and more. She is a professor at Harper College, a community college in suburban Chicago, where she lives with her husband and daughter.

Brit Washburn studied creative writing at Interlochen Arts Academy in Northern Michigan, Eugene Lang College in New York City, and Goddard College in Vermont, as well as comparative religion at the University of Hawai'i. She was twice awarded the Albion Prize for Poetry, judged by the poets Gary Snyder and Ai, and her work has appeared in numerous journals and anthologies.

Anne Williams has published short fiction and nonfiction (most recently in Cutbank), a textbook for Prentice Hall, and worked as a feature writer for *The Durango Herald* in southern Colorado. She says, "I'm currently settled on a working organic farm where I do practically none of the work but have all the fresh produce I can manage."

Gracie Yates is a 16-year-old junior at Central Hardin High School and a singer/songwriter. Most of her free time is spent writing songs and poetry, and creating music. Gracie also plays lacrosse and work as a lifeguard.

www.ingramcontent.com/pod-product-compliance
Lightning Source LLC
Chambersburg PA
CBHW071014120726
47910CB00004B/1513